Hudson Ohio

Keith Curley, Liz Murphy, and Kristina Roegner

The Wooster Book Company
where minds and imaginations meet

Wooster, Ohio   2010

ON **FRONT COVER**

A rare view from inside the Clock Tower.

PHOTO BY **TOM JONES**

ON THE **TITLE PAGE**

Ceramic tile mural of Hudson village center.

ARTWORK BY **DEBBIE CURRIN**

ON **FRONT JACKET FLAP**

The Hudson Corporation marker identifies Township 4, Range 10, of the Western Reserve, which was purchased by David Hudson of Goshen, Connecticut in 1799 for about thirty cents per acre. The town was settled by a group of about twenty-five pioneer settlers, who traveled west with David Hudson in the summer of 1800.

PHOTO BY **THOMAS MUNN**

The Wooster Book Company
205 West Liberty Street
Wooster Ohio • 44691
www.woosterbook.com

© 2010 Picture Hudson LLC. All rights reserved.

No part of this book may be reproduced, utilized, or transmitted in any form or by any means, electronic or mechanical, including photocopying, recording, scanning, or by any information storage-and-retrieval system, without permission in writing from the copyright holder.
Printed in China.

ISBN: 978-1-59098-179-5

Library of Congress Cataloging-in-Publication Data
Curley, Keith.
Hudson Ohio / Keith Curley, Liz Murphy, Kristina Roegner.
p.cm.
Includes index.
ISBN 978-1-59098-179-5 (alk. paper)
1. Hudson (Ohio)—Pictorial works.
2. Hudson (Ohio)—History.
I. Muphy, Liz, (date)   II. Roegner, Kristina.   III. Title.
F499.H8C87 2010
977.1'36—dc222010000015

for Betsy, Greg, Eric
and the people of Hudson, Ohio

In 1799, David Hudson

purchased and settled twenty-five square miles in the frontier wilderness known as the Western Reserve. He led his family and a handful of determined pioneers from Connecticut to the land which would later be named in his honor. Though Hudson was an untamed virgin forest when the settlers first arrived, twenty-seven years later in 1826 it was developed enough to be the site selected for the first college in northeastern Ohio, Western Reserve College, whose historic campus is now home to Western Reserve Academy.

David Hudson set into motion a vibrant history of a village, township, and eventually the city of Hudson, Ohio. Once part of the Underground Railroad, Hudson was home to John Brown, the famous abolitionist who led the raid on Harper's Ferry, and businessman James W. Ellsworth, who went on to become the town's benefactor. Many inventors and leaders have called Hudson home, including G.H. Grimm, who created the first evaporator for maple syrup, John Ong, CEO of B.F. Goodrich, who went on to become the U.S. Ambassador to Norway, Burton D. Morgan, who established the Burton D. Morgan Foundation with its commitment to entrepreneurialism, and Tom Murdough, who founded Little Tikes, and led the development of Hudson's downtown First & Main. What has, and continues to define Hudson, are her citizens, many of whom are dedicated to preserving Hudson's historic heritage while others energetically shape and forge ahead towards a bright future.

Nestled between Cleveland and Akron, Ohio, Hudson proudly offers families first class school systems, both public and private. Uniquely sized, Hudson is large enough to offer some of the finest restaurants in the region, yet is small enough that in the summer you will still find children selling homemade lemonade along the side of the road. Hudson is large enough to have one of the finest fire and EMS departments in the area, yet small enough that these service men and women are still volunteers. Hudson is indeed a destination, attracting thousands of visitors each year, but to those who have ever lived here, Hudson will always be home.

Welcome to Hudson.

David Hudson

HISTORICAL IMAGE COURTESY OF **TOM VINCE**

The Clock Tower has become a well recognized symbol and landmark of Hudson Ohio.

PHOTO BY **TOM JONES**

Preface

Guests visiting from Landsberg, Germany, Hudson's sister city, presented our family with a gift. The gift was a picture book of their hometown. It was beautiful, filled with pictures of structures, events, parks, and more. Leafing through the pages, I truly got a flavor of the essence of Landsberg. Hoping to reciprocate, I ran immediately to The Learnéd Owl Book Shop to find Hudson's equivalent, and found none. There were interesting books on Hudson's history but nothing quite captured the whole essence of our city—which can best be captured through photographs.

The vision for this book came together then. Let's create a hardcover, high-quality picture book to capture the character and beauty of Hudson, Ohio. Let the citizens of Hudson provide the pictures, have a jury select the ones to be included, and then donate one-hundred percent of the profits to Hudson charities. Joining together with Liz Murphy, the owner of The Learnéd Owl Book Shop, and Keith Curley, president of the Western Reserve Systems Group, LLC, the three of us established PictureHudson.

It is the citizens of Hudson who created this book. Over 150 individuals contributed the photographs, over 1300 in all were submitted. A dedicated six-member jury, comprised of Gretchen Bierbaum, Debbie Currin, Molly Logan, Pete McDonald, Kathie Rowe Franks, and Tom Vince spent many hours pouring over the photographs, deliberating and selecting the over one hundred to be included in this book. The decisions were not easy. Photographs were selected based on beauty, quality, resolution, artistic perspective, and content. The jury sought out photographs which would represent all four seasons and the many diverse aspects of Hudson and I believe they have accomplished just that.

These exquisite photographs should remind us of how precious our heritage is and instill in all of us a determination to leave Hudson in as good a condition as we found it—or to make it even better. I hope you enjoy this photographic journey through Hudson and come to love our community as deeply as I do.

—KRISTINA DALEY ROEGNER

This view looks across The Green toward the Clock Tower and Hudson's historic Main Street buildings. Hudson's Clock Tower, built in 1913, was a gift to the community from benefactor James W. Ellsworth.

PHOTO BY **MICHELE DILLON MONCRIEF**

Detail of the door on the Hudson Clock Tower.

PHOTO BY **MICHAEL QUIGLEY**

Ice sculpture of Clock Tower at the First & Main Winter Festival.

PHOTO BY **MATT GREENE**

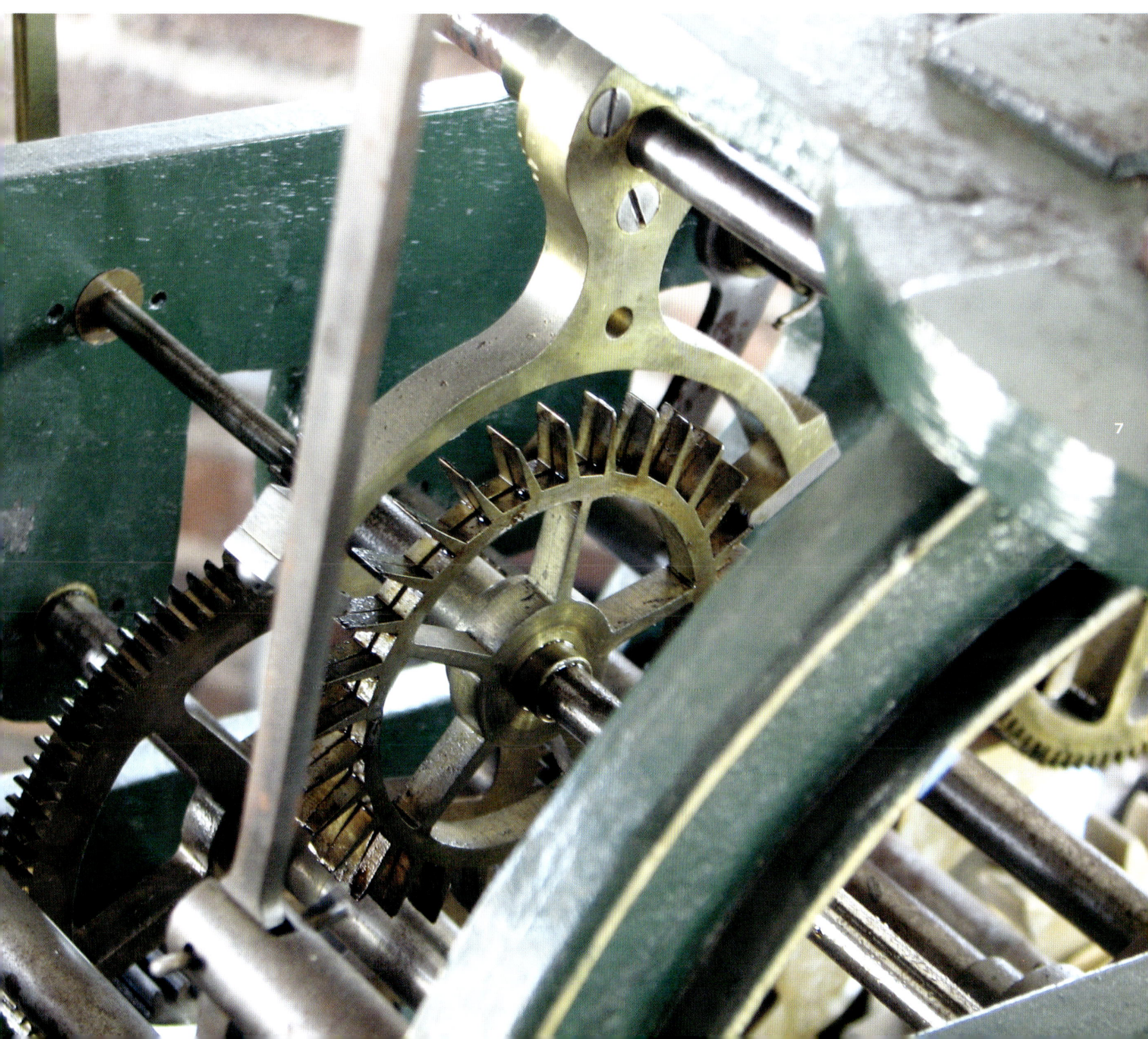

Detail of mechanical clockworks of Hudson's Clock Tower

PHOTO BY **ERIK BREEDON**

The Old Hudson Township Burying Ground
on Chapel Street is Hudson's oldest
cemetery, dating from 1808
with the burial of John Brown's mother.
Most of Hudson's early pioneers are also
buried here, including David Hudson,
Owen Brown, and the Baldwins.

PHOTO BY **PATTY CLARY**

Draper Cemetery, located on State Route 303 just east of Stow Road, was originally founded as a family cemetery in 1881. The Draper Family was among Hudson's earliest pioneer families. Lora Case, the boyhood friend of John Brown, is among those buried here.
Draper is still one of three active cemeteries operated by the City of Hudson. The others are Markillie-St. Mary and O'Brien Cemeteries.

PHOTO BY **KRISTINA DALEY ROEGNER**

Hudson High School's award winning Swing Marching Band performs awe-inspiring routines not only at games but at other sporting events, competitions, and parades.

PHOTO BY **BRIAN S. SUNTKEN**

PHOTO BY **KENNETH M. KLEMENCIC**

PHOTO BY **BRIAN S. SUNTKEN**

PHOTO BY **KATHIE ROWE FRANKS**

Hudson athletes excel in every competitive sport.

PHOTOS BY **KENNETH M. KLEMENCIC**

Demonstrating the true Hudson pioneer spirit of undying fortitude, two young football players remain undaunted.

PHOTO BY **CHRISSY FUCHS**

Aspiring ballerinas and their teacher practice in their studio.

PHOTO BY **SANDY PALAZZO**

Hudson shopkeepers decorate their windows in keeping with the season, while the Western Reserve Community Band entertains shoppers during the annual Holiday Walk.

PHOTO BY MARIANNE REDSLOB

PHOTO BY **BOB ZELLER**

One of many Christmas traditions in Hudson is lighting the luminarias and adorning the trees on The Green.

PHOTO BY **TIM FENNER**

PHOTO BY **TOM JONES**

17

Loomis Observatory, built in 1838 on the campus of Western Reserve Academy, is the second oldest observatory in the United States that is still on its original foundation. The telescopes that can still be seen inside the building were purchased by Elias Loomis in Europe.

PHOTO BY **TOM JONES**

The Nathan Seymour House was built in 1843 by a classics professor at the old Western Reserve College, and now serves as the guest house for the Western Reserve Academy.

PHOTO BY **ERIK BREEDON**

Looking through the portico at Hayden Hall, the music department of the Western Reserve Academy. This building, from 1878, was originally a cheese warehouse. James W. Ellsworth had the building renovated in 1910 for use as the Hudson Club House, open to all residents of the community.

PHOTO BY **TOM JONES**

The Western Reserve Academy Chapel, built in 1836, stands at the center of the historic Brick Row. Designed as a New England style meeting house, the Chapel is still used for student gatherings, concerts, and other performances, as well as the occasional wedding and church service.

PHOTO BY **KRISTIN SHAWD**

Western Reserve Academy Brick Row is seen in front of Seymour Hall (built in 1913), the school's main classroom building. John Pierce, a graduate of WRA, did the first systematic planting of trees on this campus in 1851. Ten years later, Pierce and his brothers went west and became the founders of the city of Denver, Colorado.

PHOTO BY ERIK BREEDON

Western Reserve Academy Chapel Tower. The top segment of the tower was struck by lightning during a storm in 1869 and was removed at that time. More than one hundred years later, an exact replica of the top segment was built as a tribute to Hudson historian, Grace Goulder Izant.

PHOTO BY **BOB ZELLER**

Former Headmaster, Henry "Skip" Flanagan Jr., and students walking along Brick Row in front of the John D. Ong Library, named in honor of the President of the Board of Trustees (who retired in 1995), long-time Hudson resident, former B.F. Goodrich CEO, and former Ambassador to Norway.

PHOTO BY **DOUG GARMON,** COURTESY OF **WESTERN RESERVE ACADEMY**

The main gate of Western Reserve Academy, originally the campus of Western Reserve College (founded 1826). WRC was built when Hudson was chosen as the site of the first college in the fourteen-county area of the Western Reserve. The Academy, founded at the same time, remained in Hudson when the college moved to Cleveland in 1882. Hudson benefactor, James W. Ellsworth, restored the historic buildings and eventually endowed the school.

PHOTOS BY **PATTY CLARY** (right) and **CHRISSY FUCHS** (right, over)

Old Tannery Farm, on Hines Hill Road, was established as a homestead and tannery by abolitionist leader John Brown in 1818. The original house that he built for his young family in 1824 is still privately owned. John Brown later won fame and notoriety for his raid on Harper's Ferry in 1859.

PHOTOS BY **CAROLE P. SMITH** (top left) and **KEITH CURLEY** (top right)

Hudson's connection with Landsberg, Germany began with a Hudson soccer team's visit and an invitation to become an exchange partner. In 1984, Hudson and Landsberg agreed to officially become "sister cities."

PHOTO BY **JACKIE SMITH** (bottom right)

Downtown Hudson's historic Main Street has been lined with local merchants since 1812. After a fire, the Main Street buildings between Park Lane and Clinton Street were rebuilt in the 1890s. The buildings north of Clinton, spared from the fire, date from the 1840s.

PHOTOS BY **MATT GREENE** (top) and **REGAN GETTENS** (left)

The merchants of Hudson, some of whom have been in the same Main Street locations for over half a century, are the heart of a vibrant downtown community. With this group as a core, Hudson has become a travel destination for people seeking excellence in shopping, theater, arts, dining, and more.

PHOTOS BY **BOB ZELLER** (left) and **SHEILA PACKARD** (right, over)

The downtown shopping district was expanded in 2004 with the construction of First & Main. Much care was taken to ensure that this new area would complement and blend seamlessly with Hudson's historic Main Street. A section of First Street is paved with historic bricks rescued from Fairport Harbor on Lake Erie.

PHOTOS BY **KENNETH M. KLEMENCIC** (left) and **BOB SENUTA** (below)

Throughout Hudson, local and national chains and independent merchants work together to make Hudson attractive and inviting for all visitors.

PHOTOS BY **THOMAS MUNN** (top left), **REGAN GETTENS** (bottom left), and **JOHANNA WOOLDREDGE** (right)

A determined shopper is undeterred by three feet of snow.

PHOTO BY **JACK RIGBY**

Turner's Mill was built in 1854 by Edgar B. Ellsworth as a lumber mill and operated as such into the twentieth century. Turner's Mill, located on State Route 303, now houses a restaurant and offices.

PHOTO BY TOM JONES

This hand pumper, originally purchased in March of 1859, was the first fire engine in all of Summit County. When Hudson's fire bell rang, the first horse team to get to the pumper pulled it to the fire (the horse team owner was paid fifty cents). If no horse team showed up, it was pulled by hand. It was last used in 1911, and donated to the Summit County Historical Society in the 1940s. The pumper was seriously damaged when the building housing it caught fire in 1963. Bill Varnes, then a Lieutenant in Hudson's fire department, refurbished it in his garage with the help of HFD members. First displayed to the public again during the 1964 Memorial Day parade, this antique is kept in working order at the Hudson Fire Department's museum room.

PHOTOS BY **RON ZENDARSKI** (left) and **KENNETH M. KLEMENCIC** (right, over)

The Hudson Train Depot dates to the early twentieth century. Hudson was the first community in Summit County to have train service with the arrival of the Cleveland-Pittsburgh Railroad in 1851. The first Hudson depot, where Abraham Lincoln's inaugural train stopped in 1861, was located near the present Hudson police station.

PHOTO BY **MARTIN OLSEN**

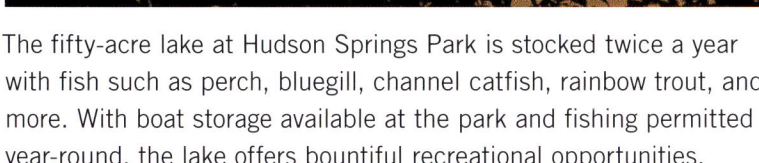

The fifty-acre lake at Hudson Springs Park is stocked twice a year with fish such as perch, bluegill, channel catfish, rainbow trout, and more. With boat storage available at the park and fishing permitted year-round, the lake offers bountiful recreational opportunities.

PHOTOS BY **TOM JONES** (above) and **BILL CURRIER** (below)

Sunrise at Hudson Springs Park.

PHOTO BY **TOM JONES**

Two generations set off together on a lake kayak adventure. Hudson is a family friendly community which caters to diverse interests and hobbies.

PHOTO BY JACK RIGBY

Hudson Springs Park, 260 acres located off Stow Road, is one of Hudson's most popular parks. It was purchased by the City of Hudson from the May family in two parcels in 1975 and 1978. Hudson Springs Park offers a 1.8-mile hiking trail around the lake, multiple pavilions, a large playground, disc golf course, fishing, boating, and of course opportunities to relax and commune with nature.

PHOTOS BY **WILLIAM DICKINSON** (left) and **THOMAS REED** (above)

On a chilly morning in May at Hudson Springs Park, a gaggle of Canada geese enjoy a leisurely swim as the mist rises on the fifty-acre lake. With all of its natural beauty, Hudson Springs Park is truly a jewel of Hudson.

PHOTO BY **ERIC HUTCHINSON**

Foliage, set ablaze with fall colors, provides a scenic backdrop to the canoe rack at Hudson Springs Park.

PHOTO BY **JACK RIGBY**

The boardwalk over the water connects walking paths at Barlow Community Center while a blue heron keeps watch underneath.

PHOTO BY **JACK RIGBY** (left)

A Canada goose floats along one of Hudson's many protected wetland areas.

PHOTO BY **TOM JONES**

Hudson is blessed with many beautiful parks. Cascade Park is seventy-five acres and offers scenic hiking trails, baseball fields, playgrounds, and more. The waterfall, pictured here, can be found along the hiking path. The boardwalk bridge connects Cascade Park with Nicholson Drive.

PHOTOS BY **KERRY PALUSCSAK** (above), and **JACK RIGBY** (opposite)

An open gate welcomes visitors to Hudson's annual Home and Garden Tour which has been sponsored by the Hudson Garden Club since 1947.

PHOTO BY **BOB ZELLER** (top)

A plein-air artist paints during the ice-cream social, one of the festivities surrounding the Home and Garden Tour.

PHOTO **KRISTINA DALEY ROEGNER** (bottom)

A garden in full bloom welcomes those on the Home and Garden tour to "Thistle Cottage" located on Manor Drive.

PHOTO BY HELEN STRONG

One of the many charming houses on Division Street, this brick house, built by John Nutting Farrar in 1844, was the home of the Trumbull family for several decades. The Trumbull family was the donor of Hudson's Trumbull Woods Park on Middleton Road.

PHOTO BY ELISABETH STONE

A beautiful Hudson residential street is blanketed in winter snow.

PHOTO BY PATTY CLARY

The Lighton Barn on Main Street dates from about 1878 and was built by the Lighton family who owned the property for fifty-one years. The barn adds character to the northern entrance into downtown Hudson and is a favorite subject for local artists.

PHOTO BY **GRETCHEN CANTONI**

A PAINTING OF THE LIGHTON BARN BY LOCAL HUDSON ARTIST **GRETCHEN BIERBAUM**.

The David Hudson house is the oldest house still on its original foundation in Hudson, in Summit County, and in the fourteen county area of the Western Reserve. The house remained in the Hudson family until 1968, when it was purchased by Western Reserve Academy for use as a faculty residence. The Hudson Heritage Association is the group charged with issuing the official markers for historic buildings as shown here.

HISTORICAL IMAGE COURTESY OF **TOM VINCE**

PHOTO BY **CHRISSY FUCHS** (below)

Hudson residents love their pets! Two fluffy canines keep watch over and welcome visitors to their home.

PHOTO BY ELISABETH STONE

A straight and narrow wrought iron fence is one of many beautiful architectural details adding character to Hudson.

PHOTO BY ELISABETH STONE

Time seems to stand still on the porch at the Hanna Hurn house (1835) on Church Street, another street in the old village filled with architecturally beautiful homes.

PHOTO BY MATT GREENE (right)

The Grissom House, originally located where the Hudson High School is today, was moved in 1984 to this location on Owen Brown Street by the Hudson Heritage Association and Katie Coulton.

PHOTO BY MATT GREENE

Another inviting porch in Hudson's historic district.

PHOTO BY **MATT GREENE**

A cyclist relaxes on a welcoming tree-lawn.

PHOTO BY **BOB ZELLER**

This Colonial Revival House at 52 Aurora Street was built in the 1920s.

PHOTO BY **KATHIE ROWE FRANKS**

The Whedon-Farwell House, built in 1826, at 30 Aurora Street is considered a masterpiece by early Hudson architect, Lemuel Porter. Built by Benjamin Whedon, who came to Hudson in 1805, this house served as a young ladies' seminary in the nineteenth century and was the location of the privately operated Hudson Primary School in the 1930s. It was extensively restored in the late 1990s.

PHOTO BY **KENNETH M. KLEMENCIC**

A view from the sidewalk on College Street looking toward Hayden Hall, now the music department of Western Reserve Academy. Built in 1878, this building was originally the Straight and Son Cheese Warehouse.

PHOTO BY **NICK ZAKLANOVICH**

This elaborate Queen-Anne style house from the 1880s, located at 35 Church Street, was built by Hudson merchant Charles Buss. Its distinctive architectural detail is the pyramidal-roofed tower on the corner of the house.

PHOTO BY **CINDY BEIDLER**

The Brewster Store (built in 1839) is one of the oldest commercial buildings in the fourteen county area of the Western Reserve. Built by Anson Brewster and his business partner, Zenas Kent, for use as a store, the building has long been home to a bank. This handsome building is an example of Federal Style architecture and may have been modeled after a building in Boston designed by Charles Bullfinch. Brewster built his imposing mansion directly next door, which the Brewster family continued to occupy until the turn of the twentieth century.

PHOTO BY ERIK BREEDON

PHOTO BY **KATHIE ROWE FRANKS**

The outskirts of Hudson still retain a rural feel, with several farms and larger estates including these pictured here.

PHOTO BY TOM JONES

Hudson Town Hall at the corner of East Main and Church streets, was the original location of the First Congregational Church (1820–1865). Erected in 1879, the Hudson Town Hall was built to house the government offices for both Hudson Village and Hudson Township which included police and fire departments. A separate addition was built in 1896 to house the fire department equipment.

PHOTOS BY **SCOTT ANDERSON** (left) and **TOM JONES** (right)

A view looking up Aurora Street at Christ Church Episcopal and the First Congregational Church.

PHOTO BY **ELIZABETH OSBORNE**

Christ Church Episcopal, founded in 1842, was originally a Gothic-Revival style building on this site. It was then replaced in 1930 with this Colonial-Revival style church. Next door is the classically styled Isham Beebe House built in 1834 and designed by noted Hudson architect and builder, Leander Starr. This building, known today as the Guildhall, is part of the Christ Church complex.

PHOTO BY **KENNETH M. KLEMENCIC** (opposite top)

A view of Aurora Street looking west at the Christ Church Episcopal, the Brewster Mansion (built in 1853) and the Brewster Store (built in 1839).

PHOTO BY **ELIZABETH OSBORNE** (opposite bottom)

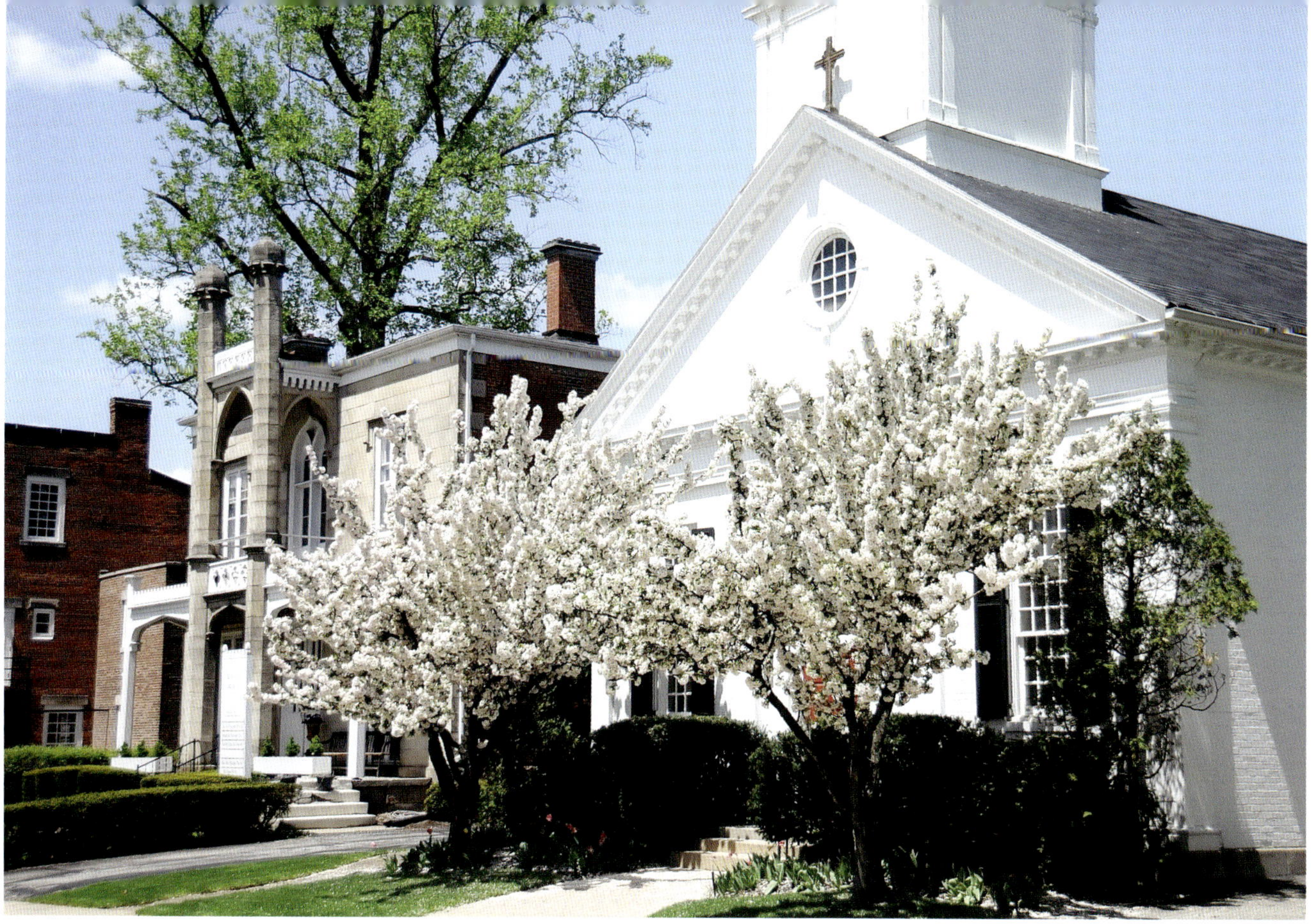

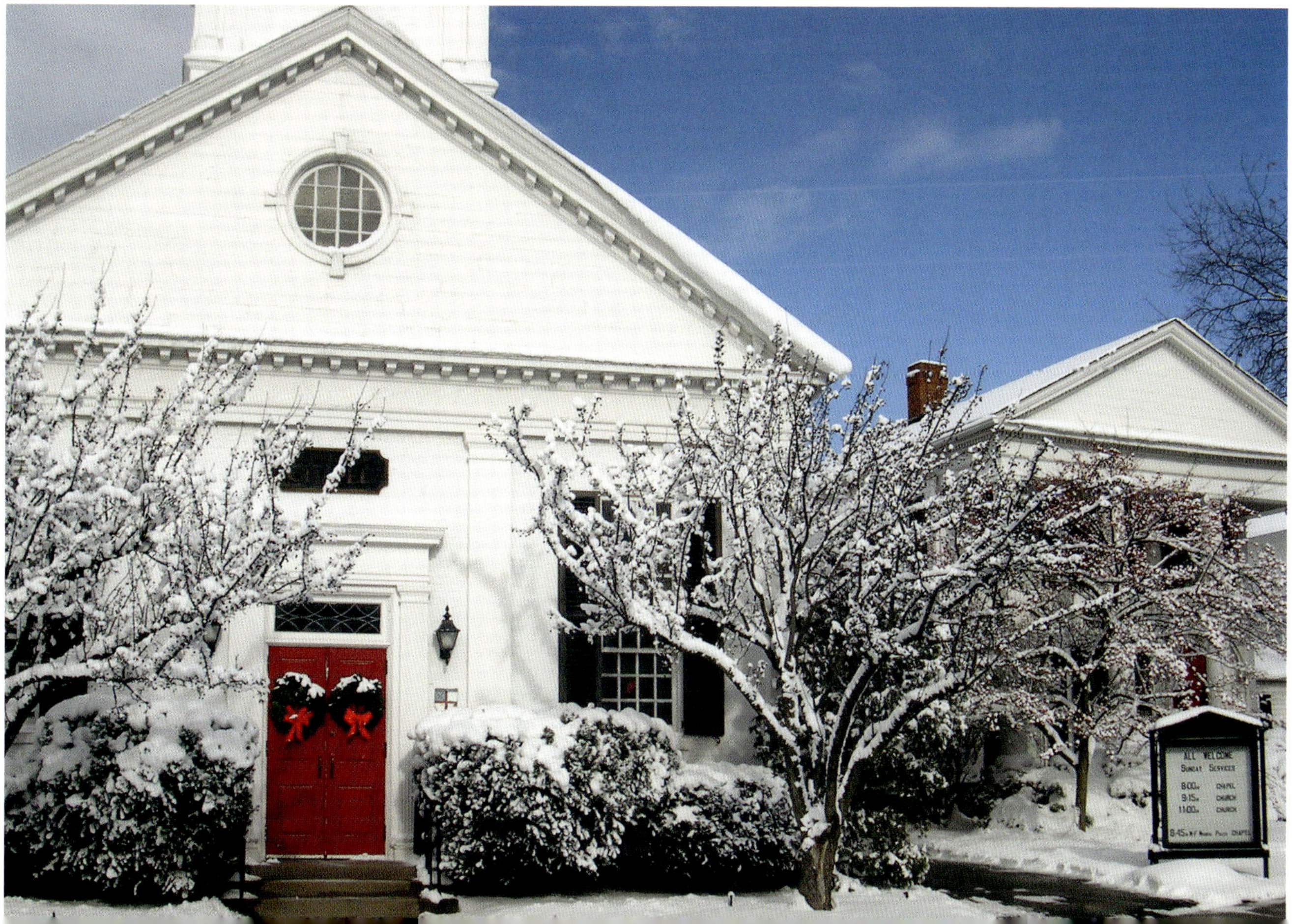
ALL WELCOME
SUNDAY SERVICES
8:00 CHAPEL
9:15 CHURCH
11:00 CHURCH

First Congregational Church on Aurora Street is the oldest church in Hudson. Founded in 1802 by Deacon David Hudson, the church was originally located on The Green. This large Romanesque-style church was built during the Civil War. It was dedicated in 1865.

PHOTO BY **MICHELE DILLON MONCRIEF**

The Old Church on The Green (*opposite*) was the original home of Saint Mary Parish. The original structure (built in 1860) was moved from Railroad Street, now Maple Drive, to this location in 1890 and extensively renovated. Saint Mary Parish then used the building until 1970, after which it became privately owned and is a multi-purpose building.

PHOTO BY **BIRGIT RHOADS**

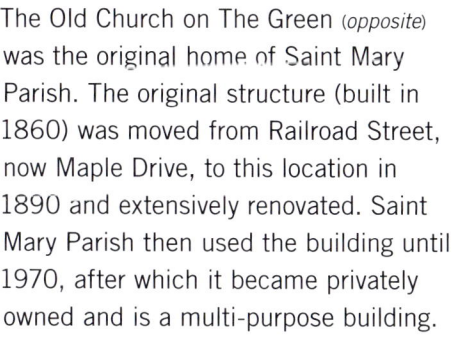

The Hudson Bandstand built in 1976 and located on The Green, is the third bandstand that Hudson has had since the late 1880s. Designed by Hudson architect Richard Derr, the bandstand is the site of summer concerts on The Green, weddings, and other civic ceremonies. Like the Clock Tower, the bandstand has become a recognized symbol of Hudson.

PHOTOS BY **JAMES D. TROXELL** (above left), **SCOTT ANDERSON** (above right), **ELIZABETH OSBORNE** (below right), and **TOM JONES** (below left)

PHOTO BY TIM FENNER

Barlow Farm Park showing its distinctive red barn (built in 1890) at the Case Barlow Farm is located on Barlow Road. This barn has long been a favorite subject for local artists. The original farm of 418 acres was later divided and twenty-two acres donated to the community in the late 1990s.

PHOTO BY **NICOLE ARIGO**

The Water Tower (opposite), which can be seen from Veterans Way, is one of several water towers serving the community.

PHOTO BY **DAVID ALAN**

71

This stained glass window of the Clock Tower was created by Hudson craftsman, Peter McDonald for the Markillie-St Mary's cemetery chapel.

PHOTO BY **HELEN STRONG**

The Baldwin House (built in 1834) on East Main Street was built by Hudson merchant Frederick Baldwin, whose daughter, Caroline Baldwin Babock, was born in this house. She later founded the Hudson Library and Historical Society, which used this building from 1925 until 2005. The house was extensively restored by the Burton D. Morgan Foundation and is currently the home of the Hudson Community Foundation and three other non-profit community groups.

PHOTO BY **KRISTINA DALEY ROEGNER**

Hudson is recognized nationally for its excellent school systems, both public and private (pictured top to bottom: Hudson Montessori School, Ellsworth Hill Elementary, Seton Catholic School; opposite bottom left, Hudson Middle School).

PHOTOS BY **MICHELLE LEZOR** (top), **DENISE LUKINGBEAL** (middle), **PATRICIA FRITZ** (below), and **KERRY PALUSCSAK** (opposite bottom left)

Two boys await the approach of the Hudson City School bus. A girl crosses the street on her bicycle under the watch of Clark Rumiser, who has served as crossing guard in Hudson for more than thirty years.

PHOTOS BY **JULIE CLARK ROBINSON** (above) and **KATHY SUNTKEN** (below)

A scene of sunflowers at the Grissom Farm on Hudson-Aurora Road, now the site of the Hudson High School. The new high school at Hudson-Aurora Road and Stow Road was opened in 1991.

PHOTOS BY **GINNY HENDERSHOTT** (left) and **KENNETH M. KLEMENCIC** (below)

To the delight of children and adults alike, the Merchants of Hudson offer trick-or-treating downtown. An annual art contest encourages young artists to decorate shop windows for the holiday.

PHOTO BY **KENNETH M. KLEMENCIC**

The Boy Scout Cabin on the Southwest Green is the home of Boy Scout Troop #321. It was built in 1931 by The Rotary Club of Hudson who officially sponsors the troop.

PHOTOS BY **TOM JONES** (above) and **CULLEN TAUSSIG** (right)

The Hudson Library and Historical Society was founded in 1910. They built this large and imposing building in the First & Main area and opened their doors in 2005.

PHOTOS BY **REGAN GETTENS** (left) and **CHRIS JORDAN** (above)

The Hudson Farmers Market, started by a Leadership Hudson Class in 2007, is held on The Green by the Clock Tower every Saturday morning from mid-summer to early fall. Residents flock to The Green to buy fresh produce from local vendors.

PHOTOS BY **KATHLEEN HARRINGTON** (opposite above), **KRISTINA DALEY ROEGNER** (opposite below), **STACY SCHURMAN PHOTOGRAPHY** (above left), and **JOHANNA WOOLDREDGE** (above right)

Christmas on Lake Forest.

PHOTO BY **ANNE MACWHERTER**

Lake Forest Country Club (built in 1929) is an example of a stately Tudor Revival building. It was originally intended to be the centerpiece of an upscale residential area where the houses would all reflect the Tudor style. With the Great Depression, the Country Club and its adjacent development went bankrupt and the mortgage was not lifted until the late 1940s. Along with the Hudson Country Club and Ellsworth Meadows, Lake Forest Country Club offers excellent golfing opportunities.

PHOTO BY **TOM JONES**

Taste of Hudson draws tens of thousand of visitors each Labor Day weekend, inviting people to sample the best culinary delights that Hudson has to offer. Taste of Hudson is one of many annual events drawing visitors to Hudson.

PHOTO BY **BRIAN S. SUNTKEN**

Pedestrian-friendly Hudson, Ohio welcomes bicyclists and walkers to its downtown business district.

PHOTO BY ERIK BREEDON

The Memorial Day parade down Hudson's Main Street has been a special feature of community life for several decades. The parade begins near Hudson Plaza on State Route 303 and marches north along Main Street to the Markillie-St. Mary Cemetery for a memorial ceremony honoring veterans.

PHOTOS BY **TIM FENNER** (above), **BRIAN S. SUNTKEN** (right), and **KATHIE ROWE FRANKS** (opposite top), **CAITLIN WILSON** (opposite bottom)

Each year Hudson's vibrancy is captured in the Fourth of July fireworks. A spectacular display of lights draws visitors from near and far.

PHOTOS BY **RON ZENDARSKI** (left) and **KENNETH M. KLEMENCIC**

Special thanks to all those who made this book possible:

- to the residents of Hudson who submitted over 1300 photographs! They were all beautiful;

- to the jury who put in countless hours reviewing each photograph and their invaluable input to the photo selection and layout: Gretchen Bierbaum, Debbie Currin, Kathie Rowe Franks, Molly Logan, Peter McDonald, and Tom Vince;

- to Western Reserve Printing at 218 North Main Street, Hudson, Ohio for their support in printing the pictures for the jury review;

- to Den Rich for his support of the project and promotion on Hudson Cable TV;

- to Mary L'Hommedieu for her legal support;

- to Bill Currin, Mayor, City of Hudson, Eric Hutchinson, and Tom Vince for their input on the text.

Index of Photographers

Alan, David   71
Anderson, Scott   62, 68
Arigo, Nicole   70
Beidler, Cindy   58
Bierbaum, Gretchen   50
Breedon, Erik   7, 19, 22, 59, 85
Cantoni, Gretchen   50
Clary, Patty   8, 24, 49
Curley, Keith   26
Currier, Bill   37
Currin, Debbie   title page
Dickinson, William   39
Fenner, Tim   17, 69, 86
Franks, Kathie Rowe   11, 56, 60, 87
Fritz, Patricia   74
Fuchs, Chrissy   14, 25, 51
Garmon, Doug   24
Gettens, Regan   27, 31, 79
Greene, Matt   6, 27, 53, 54, 55
Harrington, Kathleen   80
Hendershott, Ginny   76
Hutchinson, Eric   39
Jones, Tom   front cover, 2, 17, 18, 20, 33, 37, 43, 61, 63, 68, 78, 83
Jordan, Chris   79
Klemencic, Kenneth M.   10, 12, 13, 30, 35, 57, 65, 76, 77, 89
Lezor, Michelle   74
Lukingbeal, Denise   74
MacWherter, Anne   82
McDonald, Peter   72
Moncrief, Michele Dillon   4, 67
Munn, Thomas   front jacket flap, 31
Olsen, Martin   36
Osborne, Elizabeth   64, 65, 68
Packard, Sheila   29
Palazzo, Sandy   15
Paluscsak, Kerry   44, 75
Quigley, Michael   5
Redslob, Marianne   16
Reed, Thomas   39
Rhoads, Birgit   66
Rigby, Jack   32, 38, 40–41, 42, 45
Robinson, Julie Clark   75
Roegner, Kristina Daley   9, 46, 73, 80
Schurman Photography, Stacy   81
Senuta, Bob   30
Shawd, Kristin   21
Smith, Carole P.   26
Smith, Jackie   26
Stone, Elisabeth   48, 52
Strong, Helen   47, 72
Suntken, Brian S.   10, 11, 84, 86
Suntken, Kathy   75
Taussig, Cullen   78
Troxell, James D.   68
Vince, Tom   1, 51
Wilson, Caitlin   87
Wooldredge, Johanna   31, 81
Zaklanovich, Nick   57
Zeller, Bob   17, 23, 28, 46, 55
Zendarski, Ron   34, 88

Index of Subjects

Barlow Community Center   42
Cascade Park   44, 45
Cemetaries   8, 9
Churches   63–67
Clocktower   2–7, 72
Community Events   80, 81, 84–89
Gazebo   68, 69
Home and Garden Tour   46, 47
Hudson Fire Dept.   34, 35
Hudson Springs Park   37–41, 43
Hudson Train Depot   36
Outskirts/Rural Hudson   60, 61, 70, 71, 76, 82, 83
Residences   48–58, 73
Schools   10–15, 74–76
Town center/The Green   16, 17, 26–33, 59, 62, 77–79
Western Reserve Academy   18–25